The Rescue

Experiencing God's Story Series

The Story Begins: The Authority of the Bible, the Triune God, the Great and Good God

The Hero Who Restores: Humanity, Satan and Sin, Jesus Christ

The Rescue: Salvation, the Holy Spirit, the Church

New People Forever: Transformation, Mission, the End

Experiencing God's Story #3

The Rescue

Salvation, the Holy Spirit, the Church

J. Scott Duvall

Kregel Publications

CONTENTS

I would like to thank the following people for their help in developing this resource: Brandon O'Brien, Josh and Jill McCarty, Michael and Terese Cox, Julie (Byrum) Stone, Kristine (Lewis) Smith, and Brandon Holiski. The other pastoral leaders at Fellowship Church—Scott Jackson, Neal Nelson, and Darrell Bridges—have been very encouraging throughout the process. My daughter Meagan spent hours sitting in my office punching holes in each page and compiling the first round of books. Thanks, everyone!

Read Me First

Whether you were raised in the church and accepted Christ as your personal savior at age five, or whether you have only recently given your life to Christ, spiritual growth is not optional. God expects his children to *grow up!*

We define *spiritual formation* as the process of allowing God to conform us to the image of Jesus Christ. The Bible clearly teaches that God wants his children to grow to maturity. As you read the sampling of verses below, especially notice the italicized words.

> For those God foreknew he also predestined to be *conformed to the likeness of his Son*, that he might be the firstborn among many brothers. (Rom. 8:29)

> Therefore, I urge you, brothers, in view of God's mercy, to offer your bodies as living sacrifices, holy and pleasing to God—this is your spiritual act of worship. Do not conform any longer to the pattern of this world, but *be transformed* by the renewing of your mind. Then you will be able to test and approve what God's will is—his good, pleasing and perfect will. (Rom. 12:1–2)

> And we, who with unveiled faces all reflect the Lord's glory, are *being transformed into his likeness* with ever-increasing glory, which comes from the Lord, who is the Spirit. (2 Cor. 3:18)

> Therefore we do not lose heart. Though outwardly we are wasting away, yet inwardly *we are being renewed* day by day. (2 Cor. 4:16)

> My dear children, for whom I am again in the pains of childbirth *until Christ is formed in you* . . . (Gal. 4:19)

> You were taught, with regard to your former way of life, to put off your old self, which is being corrupted by its deceitful desires; to *be made new* in the attitude of your minds; and to put on the new self, *created to be like God* in true righteousness and holiness. (Eph. 4:22–24)

. . . being confident of this, that *he who began a good work in you will carry it on to completion* until the day of Christ Jesus. (Phil. 1:6)

Therefore, my dear friends, as you have always obeyed—not only in my presence, but now much more in my absence—continue to *work out your salvation* with fear and trembling, *for it is God who works in you* to will and to act according to his good purpose. (Phil. 2:12–13)

Have nothing to do with godless myths and old wives' tales; rather, *train yourself to be godly.* (1 Tim. 4:7)

Like newborn babies, crave pure spiritual milk, so that by it *you may grow up in your salvation*, now that you have tasted that the Lord is good. (1 Peter 2:2–3)

Each aspect of our definition of *spiritual formation* is significant. Spiritual formation is a *process*. We don't experience growth as a neat, clean, upward slope toward heaven. In reality it looks and feels more like a roller-coaster ride, twisting and turning and looping and climbing and dropping. Only as you stand back and see the big picture can you tell that the "exit" to the ride is higher than the "entrance." Spiritual formation is a messy process. Because we don't always cooperate with the Lord, it takes time for him to accomplish his purpose in our lives. Philippians 1:6 offers a great deal of encouragement here (see above). God never stops working.

Spiritual formation is the process of *allowing* God to work in our lives. God is sovereign but he has also created us to make important decisions and to bear the responsibility for those decisions. We have no power in and of ourselves to cause our own growth, nor will God force us to obey him. We must allow God to work in our lives and to bring about change. God deeply desires to work, but we must give him the necessary time and space. We don't cause our own growth, but we do cooperate with God as he works. Check out Philippians 2:12–13 above.

Spiritual formation is a process of allowing *God* to work in our lives. We are told that the Holy Spirit continues the earthly ministry that Jesus began (Acts 1:1–2). God's Spirit lives within each genuine believer (1 Cor. 6:19). Our growth is not the result of special circumstances or good luck. We don't grow by our own willpower or by striving to obey the Law. We grow when we follow the Holy Spirit, who alone can produce spiritual fruit in our lives (see Gal. 5:16–23). For us to be loving, joyful, peaceful, and so on, the Holy Spirit must be allowed to do his work.

Spiritual formation is the process of allowing God *to conform us* to the image of Jesus. As much as I hate to admit it, growth means change. Like clay in the potter's hand, we are shaped and molded and conformed to a particular pattern. Change at the hand of God is sometimes painful, but it is always good. We don't always like it, but deep down we always desire it because we know it is necessary. James tells us to "consider it pure joy . . . whenever you face trials of many kinds, because you know that the testing of your faith develops perseverance" and "perseverance must finish its work so that you may be mature and complete, not lacking anything" (James 1:2–4). God loves us too much to let us stay as we are.

Finally, spiritual formation is the process of allowing God to conform us *to the image of Jesus Christ*. In Romans 8:29; 2 Corinthians 3:18; and Galatians 4:19 (see page 9), we are told that God is making us more and more like his Son. Jesus is the perfect pattern or model. He represents the goal of spiritual formation. We are not being shaped into merely religious people or ethical people or church-going people. We are being conformed to the very character of Christ himself.

Everyone, without exception, experiences some kind of "spiritual formation." Dallas Willard puts it this way:

> All people undergo a process of spiritual formation. Their spirit is formed, and with it their whole being. . . . Spiritual formation is not something just for especially religious people. No one escapes. The most hardened criminal as well as the most devout of human beings have had a spiritual formation. They have become a certain kind of person. You have had a spiritual formation and I have had one, and it is still ongoing. It is like education: everyone gets one—a good one or a bad one. (*Renovation of the Heart*, 45)

Everyone is being formed by certain powers after a particular pattern or model. We are blessed beyond words to be able to participate in God's design for spiritual formation.

God often uses resources to shape or mold us into conformity with Christ's character. Of course, the primary resource is God's Word, the Bible. But there are also many good and helpful supplementary resources. We certainly know that no ministry resource of any kind can ever substitute for a personal relationship with God through Jesus Christ, but God does seem to use spiritual-growth resources to help our love for him grow deeper and stronger. The Experiencing God's Story series is one particularly effective resource that God can use to help us understand and participate consistently in true, godly spiritual formation.

Believing-Behaving-Becoming

Most resources focus on just one aspect of the spiritual formation process. Some tools emphasize our *beliefs* by explaining the core teachings of the Christian faith. Knowing what to believe is crucial, but there is more. Many spiritual formation resources highlight how we should *behave*. They stress the importance of spiritual disciplines such as prayer, Bible study, solitude, worship, and so on. Without a doubt God uses such disciplines to transform our lives, but the disciplines are means to an end, not the end themselves.

The disciplines are like workout routines pointing toward the game itself. The game is our life with God. Finally, there are a handful of resources that pay attention to what people are *becoming* in the entire process of spiritual formation (i.e., godly character). Most of these center on the fruit of the Spirit as the true test of spirituality, and rightly so.

The Experiencing God's Story series connects all three aspects of spiritual formation: what we believe, how we behave, and who we are becoming. All three are essential to our growth:

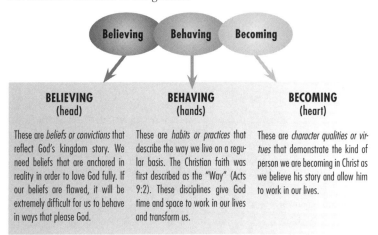

BELIEVING (head)	BEHAVING (hands)	BECOMING (heart)
These are *beliefs or convictions* that reflect God's kingdom story. We need beliefs that are anchored in reality in order to love God fully. If our beliefs are flawed, it will be extremely difficult for us to behave in ways that please God.	These are *habits or practices* that describe the way we live on a regular basis. The Christian faith was first described as the "Way" (Acts 9:2). These disciplines give God time and space to work in our lives and transform us.	These are *character qualities or virtues* that demonstrate the kind of person we are becoming in Christ as we believe his story and allow him to work in our lives.

As a teaching tool, each workbook in this series connects a "Believing" area with a "Behaving" area and a "Becoming" area. Look at the overview on pages 16–17 to see the whole plan. For example, in the third row of the overview you will notice a belief in a great and good God. That belief is connected to the habit of worship and to the quality of purity or holiness. In other words, each row of the overview is connected and integrated; each belief is tied to a behavior or habit and then to a character quality.

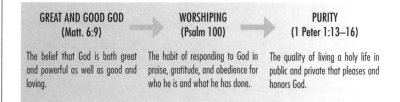

GREAT AND GOOD GOD (Matt. 6:9)	WORSHIPING (Psalm 100)	PURITY (1 Peter 1:13–16)
The belief that God is both great and powerful as well as good and loving.	The habit of responding to God in praise, gratitude, and obedience for who he is and what he has done.	The quality of living a holy life in public and private that pleases and honors God.

This Believing-Behaving-Becoming arrangement is merely a teaching tool and is not intended as a rigid religious system. Sometimes beliefs lead to behavior, while at other times behavior influences beliefs. I'm not suggesting a 1-2-3, neat, clean, foolproof, linear progression that will solve all of life's problems. We all know that life is messy, dynamic, unpredictable, confusing, spontaneous, mystical, and so on. But I still think there are important connections to be made using this teaching arrangement. For instance, what we believe about Satan and sin will affect how we fight spiritual battles and how we understand and experience true freedom. While recognizing this somewhat artificial organization, I hope the Believing-Behaving-Becoming setup encourages you to allow the Lord to work in your entire life rather than just one area of your life.

The four study guides in this series include a total of thirty-six boxes of beliefs, behaviors, and character qualities.

Why these particular topics? Were they chosen simply because they are the most popular topics when it comes to spiritual growth? Are we looking at a random bunch of beliefs and habits and virtues all loosely connected? Actually, the topics were not chosen at random or through some popularity contest. These topics reflect God's story and in our context today we definitely need to stay anchored to God's story.

Experiencing God's Story of Life and Hope

Since the late 1960s we have been experiencing a cultural shift from modernism to postmodernism. (See Jimmy Long's excellent book *Emerging Hope* for more on this cultural change and how Christians can respond.) The modern era emphasized the individual, objective truth, words, and some kind of grand story to explain the meaning of life. By contrast, the postmodern era emphasizes community, subjective "truth," images, and the absence of any grand story to explain life. Christians can embrace some aspects of postmodernism and probably need to resist others. For instance, we can certainly celebrate the greater emphasis on community. But if we give up on a big story that explains reality, then we might as well give up on our faith.

The Christian faith is founded upon God's grand story revealed in the Bible. Postmodernism does away with all big stories that claim to explain reality, opting instead for local or small-group stories. What is true for me and my friends is what is true—period! But Christians can't abandon God's grand story or there is nothing left to believe and all hope is lost. Instead, we need to understand God's story even more and see how it connects to life and how it does us good. We would say that what is real and true is not just what my local group prefers, but what God has revealed. God's story explains life.

Spiritual formation needs to be connected to God's story or it can be manipulated to mean almost anything. In other words, we need a biblical story approach to spiritual formation. But we obviously need to do more than just "believe" the story. We need to act upon the story and allow God's story to shape our whole being. Perhaps now the title makes more sense. We need to experience (beliefs, habits, character qualities) God's story (as revealed in the Bible) of life and hope (a story that does what is best for us).

How is this story approach built into these workbooks? It's simple. If you look again at the overview you will notice that the "Believing" column is actually God's grand story.

BELIEVING	(meaning in the story)
Authority of the Bible	A trustworthy script for the story
Triune God who is Great and Good	Begins with God who is community
Humanity	God wants to share his community
Satan and Sin	Evil powers try to ruin the plan
Jesus Christ	The hero of the story
Salvation	The rescue begins
Holy Spirit	God with us until the end
The Church	The community being rescued
Transformation	God works among his children
Mission	God works through his children
The End	The end—we are with God in the new creation

The very first item in the column is the *Bible* or the script of the story. The story proper begins with *God*—who he is and what he has done. God creates *human beings* to relate to him in perfect community, but *Satan and sin* spoil God's good creation and interfere with his story. God must now attempt a rescue to save his creation. Because of his great love for us, God sent his Son *Jesus Christ* to rescue us from Satan and sin and restore us to a relationship with him. *Salvation* means that God has come to rescue us from the dark side. Through Christ, God offers us a way home. As we respond to his gracious offer by trusting him, we are adopted by God into his family. He puts his very own *Spirit* within us and incorporates us into his community. God desires to use this *new community* (called *church*) to provide us with identity, stability, and wholeness. As we eat, pray, worship, and listen to God's Word together, we begin to feel safe. We open up, revealing our joys and struggles. We discover that we can really be known and loved at the same time, rather than just one or the other. Perhaps for the first time we experience life and hope through Christ and his community. We are *transformed* into the kind of person we were created to be. Naturally, we want other people to experience this life and hope. We have a *mission*— to live out God's story in biblical community so that others can join God's community. Since it is a story of hope, God's story *ends* happily (read Rev. 21:1–4).

To summarize, the "Believing" column is God's grand story. Spiritual formation is anchored in God's story. As we move through the story (from top to bottom), each Belief area extends out (from left to right) to a Behaving and a Becoming area. In this way our whole life is being shaped by the Lord and the entire process is firmly secured to God's story.

Workbook Format

Most of the studies in these workbooks consist of the following elements:

- An introduction that explores the biblical context
- "A Closer Look," to dig deeper into a particular text
- "Crossing the Bridge," to move from the ancient world to our world
- "So What?" to apply what we have discovered in the context of biblical community
- "The Power of Words," to help you understand the meaning of words in the text
- Insightful quotes that inspire reflection and action
- Application questions for your small group
- Cross-references for more Bible exploration
- A "For Deeper Study" recommended reading list

In terms of assumptions, characteristics, and benefits, the Experiencing God's Story series is:

- theologically grounded in the evangelical Christian tradition
- spiritually integrated by connecting believing, behaving, and becoming
- academically reliable through the use of solid biblical scholarship
- pedagogically interactive without being insulting (i.e., you won't find rhetorical fill-in-the-blank questions)
- creatively designed to be used by individuals within the context of biblical community
- practically and realistically arranged into four books, each with 3 three-part chapters

Another subtle characteristic worth mentioning is that the workbooks teach by example how to do responsible Bible study. The move from context to observation to theological principle to application follows the journey model detailed in *Grasping God's Word* by Scott Duvall and Daniel Hays.

May the Lord bless you richly as you allow him to conform you to the image of Jesus Christ. I pray that the Experiencing God's Story series will serve you well on your journey.

Overview of the Experiencing God's Story Series

	BELIEVING	BEHAVING	BECOMING
The Story Begins	**Authority of the Bible** (2 Tim. 3:16–17) The belief that the Bible is God's inspired Word given to us to help us mature in our faith.	**Studying the Bible** (2 Tim. 2:15) The habit of reading, interpreting, and applying the Bible as the primary means of listening to God.	**Truth** (Eph. 4:20–25) The quality of living and speaking truthfully in a world of lies and deception.
	Triune God (Gal. 4:4–6) The belief that the Bible teaches the triune (three-in-one) nature of God.	**Fellowshiping** (Acts 2:42–47) The habit of living in authentic relationship with and dependence upon other followers of Jesus.	**Love** (1 John 4:7–8) The quality of choosing to do what God says is best for another person.
	Great and Good God (Matt. 6:9) The belief that God is both great and powerful as well as good and loving.	**Worshiping** (Psalm 100) The habit of responding to God in praise, gratitude, and obedience for who he is and what he has done.	**Purity** (1 Peter 1:13–16) The quality of living a holy life in public and private that pleases and honors God.
The Hero Who Restores	**Humanity** (Gen. 1:26–28) The belief that human beings are uniquely created in the image of God.	**Seeking the Kingdom** (Matt. 6:33) The habit of acknowledging that God is our Creator and that we are creatures intended to seek him and his purposes.	**Rest** (Matt. 11:28–30) The quality of living with a deep awareness of and contentment with God's purpose for our lives.
	Satan and Sin (Gen. 3:1–7) The belief that Satan is the leader of the opposition against God and his people, and that all human beings have a willful opposition to God's claim on their lives (sin).	**Waging Spiritual War** (Matt. 4:1–11) The habit of knowing and using appropriate strategies for fighting against the Devil, the flesh, and the world.	**Freedom** (Rom. 8:1–4) The quality of experiencing freedom from Satan's power and sin's domination and freedom for new life with God.
	Jesus Christ (John 1:1–3, 14, 18) The belief that Jesus Christ is God the Son, fully divine and fully human.	**Following** (Mark 8:34–38) The habit of daily choosing to follow Jesus Christ as Lord in every area of life.	**New Identity in Christ** (John 21:15–23) The quality of single-minded allegiance to Jesus Christ above every other competing loyalty.

BELIEVING	BEHAVING	BECOMING
Salvation (Eph. 2:8–10) The belief that salvation is by grace (source), through faith (means), for good works (result).	**Trusting and Acting** (Phil. 2:12–13) The habit of allowing God to work in our lives so that our faith results in action (not salvation by works, but true faith that works).	**Assurance** (Rom. 8:15–16) The quality of knowing (with a healthy confidence) that we belong to God.
Holy Spirit (John 14:16–17) The belief that God the Spirit continues Jesus' earthly ministry, especially that of transforming believers and empowering them to fulfill their mission.	**Walking by the Spirit** (Gal. 5:16, 25) The habit of living in dependence upon the Holy Spirit as the source of strength to resist temptation and imitate Jesus Christ.	**Fruit of the Spirit** (Gal. 5:22–24) The quality of bearing the fruit of the Holy Spirit (Christlike character qualities) in one's life.
The Church (1 Peter 2:4–10) The belief that God's people are joined together in Christ into a new community, the church.	**Serving** (Mark 10:35–45) The habit of being a servant to other members of this new community.	**Humility** (Luke 18:9–14) The quality of a servant's attitude grounded in the recognition of our status before God and our relationship to others.
Transformation (Rom. 12:1–2) The belief that we are not to be conformed to this world, but we are to be transformed into the image of Jesus Christ.	**Praying** (Matt. 6:9–13) The habit of continual communion with God that fosters our relationship and allows for genuine transformation in our lives.	**Peace** (Phil. 4:6–7) The quality of calmness and well being (vs. worry and inner turmoil) that comes as a result of our communion with God.
Mission (Matt. 28:18–20) The belief that Jesus commissioned his church to make disciples of all nations.	**Engaging the World** (Acts 1:7–8) The habit of engaging the world for the purpose of sharing the good news of Jesus Christ.	**Compassion** (Luke 10:30–37) The quality of extending love and compassion to people in need.
The End (1 Thess. 4:13–18) The belief that Jesus Christ will return to judge evil, restore his creation, and live forever in intimate fellowship with his people.	**Persevering** (Heb. 12:1–2) The habit of enduring and persisting in spite of the trials and difficulties we face in life.	**Hope** (Rom. 8:22–25) The quality of a confident expectation that in the end God will be true to his word and keep his promises.

The Rescue

New People Forever

I Boast No More

Salvation

The Danish philosopher Søren Kierkegaard tells a story about how God's love moved him to come to our rescue:

Imagine there was a king that loved a humble maiden. She had no royal pedigree, no education, no standing in the court. She dressed in rags. She lived in a shack. She led the ragged life of a peasant. But for reasons no one could ever quite figure out, the king fell in love with this girl, in the way kings sometimes do. Why he should love her is beyond explaining, but love her he did. And he could not stop loving her.

Then there awoke in the heart of the king an anxious thought. How was he to reveal his love to the girl? How could he bridge the chasm of station and position that separated them? His advisers, of course, would tell him to simply command her to be his queen. For he was a man of immense power—every statesman feared his wrath, every foreign power trembled before him, every courtier groveled in the dust at the king's voice. She would have no power to resist; she would owe him an eternal debt of gratitude.

But power—even unlimited power—cannot command love. He could force her body to be present in his palace; he could not force her love for him to be present in her heart. He might be able to gain her obedience this way, but coerced submission is not what he wanted. He longed for intimacy of heart and oneness of spirit. All the power in the world cannot unlock the door to the human heart. It must be opened from the inside. His advisers might suggest that the king give up this love, give his heart to a more worthy woman. But this the king will not do, cannot do. And so his love is also his pain. . . .

The king could try to bridge the chasm between them by elevating her to his position. He could shower her with gifts, dress her in purple and silk, have her crowned queen. But if he brought her to his palace, if he radiated the sun of his magnificence over her, if she saw all the wealth and power and pomp of his greatness, she would be overwhelmed. How would he know (or she either, for that matter) if she loved him for himself or for all that he gave her? How could she know that he loved her and would love her still even if she had remained only a humble peasant? . . .

Every other alternative came to nothing. There was only one way. So one day the king rose, left his throne, removed his crown, relinquished his scepter, and laid aside his royal robes. He took upon himself the life of a peasant. He dressed in rags, scratched out a living in the dirt, groveled for food, dwelt in a shack. He did not just take on the outward appearance of a servant, it became his actual life, his nature, his burden. He became as ragged as the one he loved, so that she could be united to him forever. It was the only way. (quoted in Ortberg, *Love Beyond Reason*, 201–2)

The grand story of Scripture begins with God—Father, Son, and Spirit—living in perfect fellowship. Because of his great love for us and his desire that we experience his perfect community, God sent his Son to rescue us from Satan and sin and to bring us into a right relationship with him. In Believing 1 we will focus on *salvation*—what God has done in Jesus Christ to draw us to himself.

The salvation that God accomplished through Christ can be summarized in two movements, *humiliation* and *exaltation*, both of which are described powerfully in Philippians 2:5–11.

HUMILIATION   **EXALTATION**

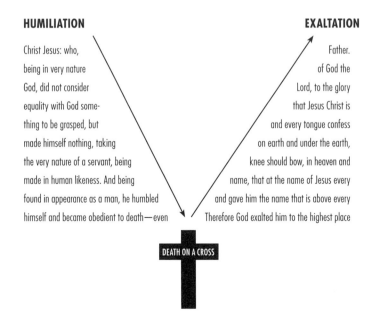

Christ Jesus: who, being in very nature God, did not consider equality with God something to be grasped, but made himself nothing, taking the very nature of a servant, being made in human likeness. And being found in appearance as a man, he humbled himself and became obedient to death—even

Father. of God the Lord, to the glory that Jesus Christ is and every tongue confess on earth and under the earth, knee should bow, in heaven and name, that at the name of Jesus every and gave him the name that is above every Therefore God exalted him to the highest place

DEATH ON A CROSS

There are many important words related to the topic of salvation. Here are just a few.

Salvation—The totality of what God has done in Christ to rescue us from sin and Satan. Salvation has three "tenses"—we *have been* saved from the penalty of sin, we *are being* saved from the power of sin, and we *will be* saved from the presence of sin.

Justification—A legal term meaning to acquit or declare a person to be just (i.e., not guilty). When we are justified, we are restored to a state of righteousness based on our trust in the grace shown us in Jesus Christ. The opposite of justification is condemnation (Rom. 8:1).

Reconciliation—This term speaks of restoring a personal relationship or renewing a friendship. When we accept Christ, we are no longer God's enemies. Rather, God adopts us as his children (John 1:12).

Redemption—This business term refers to the payment of a ransom in order to purchase a person's freedom (slavery being the original context). Jesus paid the price to ransom us from sin (Mark 10:45).

Sanctification—The process by which people who have been justified are changed and transformed into the likeness of Christ by the power of the Spirit (Rom. 12:1–2).

Glorification—The final step in salvation, when we are made like Christ and live with him forever (Phil. 3:20–21).

The Lamb of God

He was despised and rejected by men, a man of sorrows, and familiar with suffering. Like one from whom men hide their faces he was despised, and we esteemed him not. Surely he took up our infirmities and carried our sorrows, yet we considered him stricken by God, smitten by him, and afflicted. But he was pierced for our transgressions, he was crushed for our iniquities; the punishment that brought us peace was upon him, and by his wounds we are healed. We all, like sheep, have gone astray, each of us has turned to his own way; and the LORD has laid on him the iniquity of us all. He was oppressed and afflicted, yet he did not open his mouth; he was led like a lamb to the slaughter, and as a sheep before her shearers is silent, so he did not open his mouth.

—Isaiah 53:3–7

Jesus' *humiliation* involves a downward progression—he becomes a man, then a man who is a servant, then a servant-man who dies, then a servant-man who dies the most humiliating death known to humans—crucifixion. But why did Jesus have to die?

The answer relates to who we are and who God is. We are sinful, guilty people, totally unable to do anything to rescue ourselves (read Eph. 2:1–3). In contrast, God is the holy Creator and Judge who must condemn sin. And yet God loves us and desires a relationship with us. How could God act in a way that would satisfy his holy love? How could he condemn our sin *and* still have a relationship with us? God's answer was the cross! On the cross, God took the penalty for sin (death) on himself, so that we might experience his forgiveness. Jesus Christ died in our place, as our substitute. Jesus applied Isaiah 53 to himself and understood his death as a sin-bearing death (see "The Lamb of God" in the sidebar). Paul writes, "While we were still sinners, Christ died for us" (Rom. 5:8). The beauty of the cross is that Jesus took our curse (Gal. 3:13) and bore our sin (2 Cor. 5:21) so that he might set us free from sin and restore our relationship to him. As Charles Wesley wrote in his famous hymn "And Can It Be That I Should Gain?" "Amazing love! How can it be that Thou, my God, should'st died for me?"

The second movement in salvation is *exaltation*, which includes both the resurrection and the ascension. The resurrection is the cornerstone of the Christian faith. Paul is right, "If Christ has not been raised, your faith is futile; you are still in your sins" (1 Cor. 15:17). If you want to read more about the reality of the resurrection, see Lee Strobel's *The Case for the Resurrection.* If you want to dig even deeper, the definitive work is N. T. Wright's, *The Resurrection of the Son of God.* Forty days after his resurrection, Jesus ascended to the Father, where he is now seated at his right hand, crowned with glory and honor (Col. 3:1; Heb. 2:7–9) and interceding for us (Rom. 8:34; Heb. 7:25). To help us focus on the essentials of salvation, we turn to Ephesians 2:8–10.

A Closer Look—Ephesians 2:8–10

Take a minute and read Ephesians 2:1–10 to get a feel for the context. Notice how this text moves from death to life, from slavery to freedom, from self-gratification to service. It's like taking a trip from Death Valley to Mount Everest. Actually, that journey doesn't begin to compare with the reality you read about in this short paragraph. As you reflect on God's Word on page 21, look carefully at each callout box, where the meaning is explained.

God's grace is the *basis* or source of salvation.	⁸For it is by grace you have been saved,	Emphasizes the ongoing results of our salvation and could be translated, "you are saved."
Faith is not a human "work" that earns God's gift of salvation, but faith is the *means* by which we receive salvation.	through faith—and this not from yourselves,	The word "this" refers to the whole idea of salvation by grace through faith (the first part of v. 8) and not just to the word "faith." The whole thing is a "gift from God."
	it is the gift of God—⁹not by works,	
Here the word "boast" refers to an attitude of presumption and confidence before God based on our own achievements. Since salvation is a gift, who can boast?	so that no one can boast. ¹⁰For we are	"Works" refers to human effort or activities aimed at earning salvation. Salvation is "by grace," not "by works."
	God's workmanship, created in Christ Jesus	"Workmanship" refers to the work of a craftsman or artist. It is often used in the Old Testament to refer to God's work of creating the world. Believers are God's new creation, his new masterpiece.
The *goal* of being created in Christ is good works. We don't achieve salvation by good works (the basis is grace), but our salvation should result in good works.	to do good works, which God prepared	
	in advance for us to do.	We have not been saved to wait passively for heaven. God designed us to literally "walk in" good works. We walk in what God has prepared ahead of time for our present life.

Crossing the Bridge

What theological principles (applying equally to the biblical audience and to us) do you see in Ephesians 2:8–10?

- There is absolutely nothing we can do to earn or merit salvation.

- Even though God offers salvation as a gift (by grace), we still need to receive the gift through faith for it to make any difference in our lives.

-

-

So What?

1. Which "power word" in this study's sidebar (page 19) means the most to you at this point in your life? Why?

The Great Exchange

How then could God express simultaneously his holiness in judgment and his love in pardon? Only by providing a divine substitute for the sinner, so that the substitute would receive the judgment and the sinner the pardon. . . . [God] was unwilling to act in love at the expense of his holiness or in holiness at the expense of his love. So we may say that he satisfied his holy love by himself dying the death and so bearing the judgment which sinners deserved.

—John Stott, *Cross of Christ,* 134, 152

Cross-References

Mark 10:45; John 3:1–16; Rom. 3–5; 6:23; 10:8–10; 1 Cor. 15; 2 Cor. 5:11–21; Gal. 2:20; Col. 1:19–23; 1 Tim. 2:5–6; 2 Tim. 1:9–10; Heb. 7:27; 9:11–28; 1 Peter 1:18–21; 2:22–24; 3:18

For Deeper Study

Akers, John, John Woodbridge, and Kevin G. Harney. *This We Believe: The Good News of Jesus Christ for the World.* Grand Rapids: Zondervan, 2000.

Hoehner, Harold W. *Ephesians.* Grand Rapids: Baker, 2002.

Stott, John R. W. *The Cross of Christ.* Downers Grove, IL: InterVarsity Press, 1986.

Strobel, Lee. *The Case for the Resurrection.* Grand Rapids: Zondervan, 1998.

Wright, N. T. *The Resurrection of the Son of God.* Minneapolis: Fortress, 2003.

2. How has God removed our right to boast about our salvation?

3. What hits you the hardest about Christ's descent from the throne to the cross?

4. The means of experiencing salvation is faith. What is included in saving faith?

5. Do you know of any helpful illustrations that clarify the role of faith in our experience of salvation?

6. Does the fact that salvation has three tenses help you in your walk with Christ (see "Salvation" in the sidebar on page 19)? Why or why not?

7. Explain one of your theological principles (see "Crossing the Bridge" on page 21) to a group of your Christian friends.

BELIEVING 1 — *Salvation*

Working Out What God Works In

Trusting and Acting

Salvation is everything that God has done in Christ to rescue us from sin and Satan. Our focal text in the last study, Ephesians 2:8–10, shows us that salvation is *by grace* (the basis) *through faith* (the means) *for good works* (the result). As we think about how salvation is made real in our lives, the next question is this—What is the relationship between faith and works? In other words, whose job is spiritual growth? What am I supposed to do, and what should I trust God to do? Some people believe that God does it all as we simply wait on him to transform our lives. At the other extreme, you'll find people who focus almost exclusively on willpower and activity. The biblical truth lies between these two extremes of complete passivity and stubborn self-reliance. In Behaving 1 we will explore the habit of trusting and acting and how they work together to connect us to God.

The relationship between faith and works can be confusing. Consider the apparent contradiction between what Paul says and what James says:

Galatians 2:16		James 2:24
So we, too, have put our faith in Christ Jesus that we may be justified by faith in Christ and not by observing the law, because by observing the law no one will be justified.	*vs.*	You see that a person is justified by what he does and not by faith alone.

"work out"—This word means to "do" or "produce" or "accomplish" something. In the New Testament we are assured that suffering "produces" perseverance (Rom. 5:3), and we read about what Christ has "accomplished" through the apostle Paul (Rom. 15:18). The word translated "work out" here in Philippians 2 is a command. Although we can do nothing to save ourselves, we are not merely passive spectators. The Christian faith is not an "auto-pilot" kind of faith. Instead, we are to be active and involved in allowing God to do his mighty work in us.

Well, are people justified by faith or by what they do? If you read Galatians and James carefully, you will notice that the context helps to answer this question. In Galatians, Paul is facing a situation where people are thinking about replacing the gospel of grace with a false gospel based on religious works. Paul's point is that we can be justified only by relying on the work of Christ and not by trusting in our own ability. James, on the other hand, is talking to people who think that faith and works can be separated (2:18). James stresses that real faith results in good works or it is not real faith. In reality, Paul and James are like two soldiers standing back to back fighting the same enemy. You may notice as you read these two letters that both Paul and James use Abraham as an illustration of true faith (Gal. 3:6–9; James 2:21–24). Abraham trusted God and lived out that trust by his actions.

A Closer Look—Philippians 2:12–13

To get a feel for the immediate context, read a few paragraphs before and after Philippians 2:12–13, our focal passage for this study. The word "therefore" in 2:12 points back to 2:1–11 (Jesus' humiliation-exaltation), a section we considered in Believing 1.

1. Why do you suppose that 2:12–13 comes immediately after 2:1–11? What is the relationship between these two sections?

Now look carefully at the text below and highlight significant words, important commands, purpose statements (e.g., "for . . ." in v. 13), crucial prepositional phrases (e.g., "with fear and trembling"), and so on. Use the margins to make comments, show connections, or ask questions.

[12]Therefore, my dear friends, as you have always obeyed—not only in my presence, but now much more in my absence—continue to work out your salvation with fear and trembling, [13]for it is God who works in you to will and to act according to his good purpose.

Crossing the Bridge

As you cross the bridge from the ancient world to our world, what timeless theological principles do you see reflected in Philippians 2:12–13?

•

•

•

•

Partnering with God

C. S. Lewis comments on this whole issue of faith and works and Philippians 2:

> There are two parodies of the truth which different sets of Christians have, in the past, been accused by other Christians of believing. . . . One set were accused of saying "Good actions are all that matters. The best good action is charity. The best kind of charity is giving money. The best thing to give money to is the Church. So hand us over $10,000 and we will see you through." The answer to that nonsense, of course, would be that good actions done for that motive, done with the idea that Heaven can be bought, would not be good actions at all, but only commercial speculations.
>
> The other set were accused of saying, "Faith is all that matters. Consequently, if you have faith, it doesn't matter what you do. Sin away, my lad, and have a good time and Christ will see that it makes no difference in the end." The answer to that nonsense is that, if what you call your "faith" in Christ does not involve taking the slightest notice of what He says, then it is not Faith at all—not faith or trust in Him, but only intellectual acceptance of some theory about Him.
>
> The Bible really seems to clinch the matter when it puts the two things together into one amazing sentence. The first half is "Work out your own salvation with fear and trembling"—which looks as if everything depended on us and our good actions: but the second half goes on, "For it is God who works in you"—which looks as if God did everything and we nothing. . . . You see, we are now trying to understand, and to separate into water-tight compartments, what exactly God does and what man does when God and man are working together. And, of course, we begin by thinking it is like two men working together, so that you could say, "He did this bit and I

did that." But this way of thinking breaks down. God is not like that. He is inside you as well as outside. (*Mere Christianity*, 131–32)

God is at work within us, and he invites us to join him in the process. Make no mistake, spiritual growth is a lifelong process rather than a one-time event. In Philippians 3:1–14 and especially in verses 12–13 Paul talks about the process of spiritual growth. "I have not arrived," Paul says. But one thing he has learned to do—forget the past and press on toward the future that God has for him. The greatest danger as you take the journey is simply giving up or quitting. But be warned, spiritual formation is not optional. Everyone is being formed by someone or something. Because God has given us freedom, we can choose who or what will form us. Will it be the triune God who made us and loved us in Christ even while we were completely unlovable, or will it be forces opposed to God?

So What?

1. Has there ever been a time in your life when you knew that God was "at work in you"? How did you know?

2. Where and how is God at work in your life right now?

3. At this point in your life, what are the biggest obstacles to "working out your salvation" (i.e., allowing God to work in your life)?

4. What helps you "work out your salvation" without drifting into legalism? How do you *work out* your faith without that growing feeling that you have to *work for* certain things or God will no longer accept you?

5. As a community of believers, what specific things can you do to help individual members grasp and experience even more the reality of "working out your salvation"? What about the reality of God being at work in you?

6. What is the ultimate goal of spiritual growth anyway?

Jesus Loves Me, This I Know

Assurance

In the previous two parts of this chapter, we focused on the belief that salvation is by grace, through faith, for good works. We saw that this belief leads to the habit or practice of responding to God even as we trust him to work in our lives. Because God is at work in real and powerful ways, we respond to him by yielding our hearts to his leading. The Christian life cannot be reduced to willpower alone, simply gritting our teeth and trying to keep a list of laws. Neither is it entirely passive, where we sit back and "wait on God" to do it all. Genuine faith is a response to an encounter with the living God through Jesus Christ. Because we are in a new relationship, we will increasingly behave in ways that please our new Lord. Sometimes, however, our response isn't what it should be, and we begin to doubt our relationship. In Becoming 1 we turn our attention to the quality of being assured that God loves us and that we belong to God.

D o you know any insecure people? Often they are talkative, critical, even obnoxious as they clamor for other people's attention. Sometimes they are quiet, withdrawn, or sullen as they anticipate other people's disapproval. Insecure people crave affirmation and fear criticism. They will go to extremes—the latest fashion, a more expensive possession, "cynical humor," and the like—to find the love and acceptance they are so desperate for. Insecurity will stunt spiritual growth like nothing else because it eats away at the very foundation that God uses to build a life. Gordon Smith says it well.

Nothing is so fundamental to the Christian journey as knowing and feeling that we are loved. Nothing! . . . The only possible basis for growing in faith is the love of God—a love that we are sure and certain of. . . . We can find the wholeness for which we long only if we know, first, that we are loved. If this is taking a risk, it is a risk that

God will take. And there is no other foundation for spiritual growth and vitality than the confidence that we are loved. This is the gospel: God loves us. . . . Our greatest need is to know this truth and to anchor our lives to it, living in a profound inner confidence of God's love. (*Voice of Jesus*, 74, 78–79)

Insecurity is merely a symptom of a serious spiritual disease—an unwillingness to let God love us. For many of us the greatest challenge in life is accepting God's love and living securely and confidently like the child of God that we are. If you are a parent, can you imagine how you would feel if you found out one day that your children had been living in constant doubt that you really loved them? It's hard to imagine anything that would hurt more. If human parents hurt when they discover that their children don't feel their love, imagine how God must feel when we live in constant doubt about his love for us?

God desires that you have a profound confidence that you belong to him and a deep sense of security that he loves you as his precious child. Listen to God speak to your heart as you consider the following verses related to assurance:

My sheep listen to my voice; I know them, and they follow me. I give them eternal life, and they shall never perish; no one can snatch them out of my hand. My Father, who has given them to me, is greater than all; no one can snatch them out of my Father's hand. (John 10:27–29)

And hope does not disappoint us, because God has poured out his love into our hearts by the Holy Spirit, whom he has given us. You see, at just the right time, when we were still powerless, Christ died for the ungodly. Very rarely will anyone die for a righteous man, though for a good man someone might possibly dare to die. But God demonstrates his own love for us in this: While we were still sinners, Christ died for us. (Rom. 5:5–8)

Now it is God who makes both us and you stand firm in Christ. He anointed us, set his seal of ownership on us, and put his Spirit in our hearts as a deposit, guaranteeing what is to come. (2 Cor. 1:21–22)

And you also were included in Christ when you heard the word of truth, the gospel of your salvation. Having believed, you were marked in him with a seal, the promised Holy Spirit, who is a deposit guaranteeing our inheritance until the redemption of those who are God's possession—to the praise of his glory. (Eph. 1:13–14)

I pray that out of his glorious riches he may strengthen you with power through his Spirit in your inner being, so that Christ may

Amazing Love

If God is for us, who can ever be against us? Since God did not spare even his own Son but gave him up for us all, won't God, who gave us Christ, also give us everything else? Who dares accuse us whom God has chosen for his own? Will God? No! He is the one who has given us right standing with himself. Who then will condemn us? Will Christ Jesus? No, for he is the one who died for us and was raised to life for us and is sitting at the place of highest honor next to God, pleading for us. Can anything ever separate us from Christ's love? Does it mean he no longer loves us if we have trouble or calamity, or are persecuted, or are hungry or cold or in danger or threatened with death? . . . No, despite all these things, overwhelming victory is ours through Christ, who loved us. And I am convinced that nothing can ever separate us from his love. Death can't, and life can't. The angels can't, and the demons can't. Our fears for today, our worries about tomorrow, and even the powers of hell can't keep God's love away. Whether we are high above the sky or in the deepest ocean, nothing in all creation will ever be able to separate us from the love of God that is revealed in Christ Jesus our Lord.

—Romans 8:31–39 NLT

"The Spirit himself testifies with [to] our spirit"—This phrase teaches that the Holy Spirit produces the assurance that we deeply crave. The Spirit works in our hearts in ways that surpass words and go beyond logic to bring assurance that God loves us and we belong to him. The Holy Spirit is different from the spirit that condemns and enslaves us. God's Spirit is the one who gives us the inner certainty that God loves us like a perfect Father and that he will never stop loving us. As we realize once again that we belong to God, and that he has not forsaken us, we cry out, "*Abba, Father!*"

A Childlike Prayer

Take a few minutes and write a simple heart prayer to the Lord expressing how much the Spirit's assurance of God's love means to you.

dwell in your hearts through faith. And I pray that you, being rooted and established in love, may have power, together with all the saints, to grasp how wide and long and high and deep is the love of Christ, and to know this love that surpasses knowledge—that you may be filled to the measure of all the fullness of God. (Eph. 3:16–19)

In all my prayers for all of you, I always pray with joy because of your partnership in the gospel from the first day until now, being confident of this, that he who began a good work in you will carry it on to completion until the day of Christ Jesus. (Phil. 1:4–6)

That is why I am suffering as I am. Yet I am not ashamed, because I know whom I have believed, and am convinced that he is able to guard what I have entrusted to him for that day. (2 Tim. 1:12)

Therefore, brothers, since we have confidence to enter the Most Holy Place by the blood of Jesus, by a new and living way opened for us through the curtain, that is, his body, and since we have a great priest over the house of God, let us draw near to God with a sincere heart in full assurance of faith, having our hearts sprinkled to cleanse us from a guilty conscience and having our bodies washed with pure water. Let us hold unswervingly to the hope we profess, for he who promised is faithful. (Heb. 10:19–23)

Praise be to the God and Father of our Lord Jesus Christ! In his great mercy he has given us new birth into a living hope through the resurrection of Jesus Christ from the dead, and into an inheritance that can never perish, spoil or fade—kept in heaven for you, who through faith are shielded by God's power until the coming of the salvation that is ready to be revealed in the last time. (1 Peter 1:3–5)

How great is the love the Father has lavished on us, that we should be called children of God! And that is what we are! (1 John 3:1)

Dear children, let us not love with words or tongue but with actions and in truth. This then is how we know that we belong to the truth, and how we set our hearts at rest in his presence whenever our hearts condemn us. For God is greater than our hearts, and he knows everything. (1 John 3:18–20)

And this is the testimony: God has given us eternal life, and this life is in his Son. He who has the Son has life; he who does not have the Son of God does not have life. (1 John 5:11–12)

As you can tell from a brief look at only a few verses, assurance of salvation is based on what God has said (God's Word), what Jesus Christ has done (God's work), and what the Holy Spirit continues to do (God's witness). What God has promised and Christ has secured, the Spirit continues to confirm in our minds and hearts. The challenge for us is not to make ourselves feel less secure by ungodly living (the book of 1 John focuses on how a true believer will live).

A Closer Look—Romans 8:15–16

Take some time with Romans 8:15–16. Look for causes and effects, for important contrasts, and so on. Make your own notes in the margins as you dig into God's Word.

[15]For you did not receive a spirit [Holy Spirit] that makes you

a slave again to fear, but you received the Spirit of sonship.

And by him we cry, *"Abba,* Father." [16]The Spirit himself testi-

fies with [to] our spirit that we are God's children.

1. What roles does God play? What roles do we play?

2. Now read the surrounding context in your Bible (all of Romans 8). What do you see in this context that helps you understand what God is trying to say to you?

Crossing the Bridge

As you cross the bridge from the ancient world to our world, what timeless theological principles do you see reflected in Romans 8:15–16?

- When we become a Christian, we receive the Holy Spirit.

- The Holy Spirit does not promote fear and bondage but the freedom associated with being a child.

-

-

Does God Want Us to Doubt?

God wants his children to be sure that they belong to him, and does not want us to remain in doubt and uncertainty. So much so, that each of the three persons of the Trinity contributes to our assurance. The witness of God the Holy Spirit confirms the Word of God the Father concerning the work of God the Son. The three strong legs of this tripod make it very steady indeed.

—John Stott,
Authentic Christianity, 211

Cross-References

John 1:11–12; 5:24; 10:27–30; Rom. 4:16–21; 8:35–39; 2 Cor. 1:21–22; Gal. 4:4–7; Eph. 1:13–14; 3:12; 4:30; Phil. 1:3–6; 2 Tim. 1:12; Heb. 6:9–12; 10:19–23; 11:1; 1 Peter 1:3–5; 1 John 3:1, 18–24; 4:12–17; 5:11–12

For Deeper Study

Milne, Bruce. *Know the Truth.* Rev. ed. Downers Grove, IL: InterVarsity Press, 1998.

Ortberg, John. *Love Beyond Reason: Moving God's Love from Your Head to Your Heart.* Grand Rapids: Zondervan, 1998.

Smith, Gordon T. *The Voice of Jesus: Discernment, Prayer, and the Witness of the Spirit.* Downers Grove, IL: InterVarsity Press, 2003.

So What?

1. Assurance of salvation really amounts to being confident that God loves you and that you are his child. Many people believe in their heads that God loves them, but they do not feel it or sense it in their hearts. Why do you suppose this is the case?

2. What is the best advice you have ever received about accepting God's love?

3. Have you ever had negative experiences in church services where you were pressured to doubt your salvation? Now that you've had time to reflect on this experience, how do you feel about it? Was that experience helpful or harmful? Why?

4. Which of the assurance verses listed on pages 29–30 is most meaningful for you?

5. What are some things that we do as Christians to undermine our confidence that we belong to God?

6. What is one specific thing you can do this week to walk more securely and confidently in God's acceptance of you as his child?

BECOMING 1—*Assurance*

A Promise Kept

Holy Spirit

The evangelist Billy Graham has written that human beings have two great spiritual needs—one is for forgiveness, the other is for goodness. God answered our first cry at Calvary by sending his Son to take our place so that we might receive forgiveness. God heard our second cry at Pentecost by giving us his Holy Spirit, who provides the power to live a transformed life (*The Holy Spirit*, 11–12). This study targets our belief that the Holy Spirit continues what Jesus began to do during his earthly ministry—transforming us from the inside out and empowering us to fulfill our mission in this world.

In Old Testament times, people were accustomed to God living in a tabernacle or large tent (Exod. 25:8–9) and then later in a temple (1 Kings 8:13). Of course, God has never been confined to an earthly building of any kind, but that's where he allowed people to experience his presence. Throughout the Old Testament, God promised a time when he would have a closer, more personal relationship with his people. He promised a time when he would pour out his own Spirit on his people and they would know him intimately.

> I will sprinkle clean water on you, and you will be clean; I will cleanse you from all your impurities and from all your idols. I will give you a new heart and put a new *spirit* in you; I will remove from you your heart of stone and give you a heart of flesh. And I will put my Spirit in you and move you to follow my decrees and be careful to keep my laws. (Ezek. 36:25–27)

> And afterward, I will pour out my Spirit on all people. Your sons and daughters will prophesy, your old men will dream dreams, your young men will see visions. Even on my servants, both men and women, I will pour out my Spirit in those days. (Joel 2:28–29)

God began to fulfill his promise in Jesus, who came in the power of the Spirit (see Mark 1:4–8; Luke 1:35; John 1:32–34). At the close of Jesus' earthly ministry, he assured his followers that the Father would soon fulfill his promise to send the Holy Spirit. The night before he was crucified, Jesus spent the evening teaching his disciples what to expect in the days and

God's Real Temple
In the summer of 2000, Dr. Danny Hays and I led a study trip to Israel. Part of the trip included a visit to what remains of the temple in Jerusalem. At one point we took a break and sat on some old steps, one of the places where the experts told us Jesus most certainly walked. It was my turn to give a devotional thought to the group of students. As we looked around in awe at what appeared to be a holy place, I reminded them that the most holy thing they could see was not a certain wall or even the steps upon which we sat, but the people sitting next to them. Once God had a temple for his people. Now God's real temple is people, people indwelt by the Holy Spirit. As Paul says in 1 Corinthians 3:16, "Don't you know that you yourselves are God's temple and that God's Spirit lives in you [plural]?"

Pentecost?
Pentecost was originally an Old Testament festival that began on the fiftieth day after the beginning of Passover. During this celebration, people would give thanks to the Lord for the firstfruits of the early spring harvest (see Lev. 23:14–16). Christians now have the firstfruits of the Spirit as they wait for Jesus' second coming (Rom. 8:23). In the Christian calendar, Pentecost Sunday occurs on the seventh Sunday after Easter.

weeks ahead. He washed their feet and taught them to serve. He gave them a new commandment and exhorted them to love. He spoke of a vine and its branches to illustrate how to bear spiritual fruit. He warned them to expect persecution from the world. He shared a meal with them and instituted the Lord's Supper. He assured them that lasting joy and peace would replace their short-term sorrow, and he prayed for them. His words of consolation also included instructions about the Holy Spirit. Look at what Jesus said about the Holy Spirit on that extraordinary night in the Upper Room.

And I will ask the Father, and he will give you another Counselor to be with you forever—the Spirit of truth. The world cannot accept him, because it neither sees him nor knows him. But you know him, for he lives with you and will be in you. (John 14:16–17)

All this I have spoken while still with you. But the Counselor, the Holy Spirit, whom the Father will send in my name, will teach you all things and will remind you of everything I have said to you. (John 14:25–26)

When the Counselor comes, whom I will send to you from the Father, the Spirit of truth who goes out from the Father, he will testify about me. (John 15:26)

But I tell you the truth: It is for your good that I am going away. Unless I go away, the Counselor will not come to you; but if I go, I will send him to you. When he comes, he will convict the world of guilt in regard to sin and righteousness and judgment: in regard to sin, because men do not believe in me; in regard to righteousness, because I am going to the Father, where you can see me no longer; and in regard to judgment, because the prince of this world now stands condemned. I have much more to say to you, more than you can now bear. But when he, the Spirit of truth, comes, he will guide you into all truth. He will not speak on his own; he will speak only what he hears, and he will tell you what is yet to come. He will bring glory to me by taking from what is mine and making it known to you. All that belongs to the Father is mine. That is why I said the Spirit will take from what is mine and make it known to you. (John 16:7–15)

After Jesus' resurrection he reminded his disciples of the soon-to-be-fulfilled promise: "Do not leave Jerusalem, but wait for the gift my Father promised, which you have heard me speak about. For John baptized with water, but in a few days you will be baptized with the Holy Spirit" (Acts 1:4–5). In the very next chapter of Acts, we read about God keeping his promise to pour out his Spirit and live among his people in a new way. The fulfillment of the promise occurs at Pentecost.

At Pentecost, God "got out of the building" so to speak and began to live in and among his people. When asked to explain what had just happened at

Pentecost, the apostle Peter quotes Joel 2 (see page 33) as he explains that this mysterious event was God keeping his promise to live among his people in power. When people become Christ followers, God takes up residence within them in the person of the Holy Spirit. Paul summarizes:

> And you also were included in Christ when you heard the word of truth, the gospel of your salvation. Having believed, you were marked in him with a seal, the promised Holy Spirit, who is a deposit guaranteeing our inheritance until the redemption of those who are God's possession—to the praise of his glory. (Eph. 1:13–14)

Notice what is involved in this single, complex, life-changing event:

1. We hear the word of truth, the gospel.
2. We believe (faith).
3. We are included in Christ.
4. We are marked in Christ with a seal, the promised Holy Spirit (the deposit).

When we receive Christ, we receive the Holy Spirit. As Paul says in Romans 8:9: "And if anyone does not have the Spirit of Christ, he does not belong to Christ." Just as we are given new life by the Spirit at conversion (John 3:8), so we must continue to live by the Spirit (Gal. 3:2–3). The Spirit supplies boldness to witness, helps us say "no" to temptation, and produces spiritual fruit in our lives (e.g., love, joy, peace, patience). The Spirit assures us that we belong to Christ, makes us more like Christ, inspires true worship, convicts us of sin, guides us in making decisions, forms us into a community, and gifts us to minister to others. God actually lives in us by his Spirit. The Spirit guarantees that one day we will live in the very presence of God in the new heaven and new earth (see Rev. 21:3, 22; 22:3–4).

A Closer Look—John 14:16–17

Read our focal passage carefully. Identify the actions of different groups (Father, Son, Spirit, God's people, the world). Look for contrasts, reasons, promises, and relationships. Mark up the text below with your observations.

THE POWER OF WORDS

"another"—There are two common Greek words for "another"—one meaning another of the same kind, and one meaning another of a different kind. In Galatians, Paul rebukes the Galatians for chasing after "another" (or a different) gospel (Gal. 1:6–7). In John 14, Jesus assures his disciples that although he is leaving them, he will send them "another" Counselor, another of the same kind, who will live in each of them and substitute for Jesus' physical presence.

"Counselor"—The Greek word, *paraklētos*, refers to "one who is called alongside to encourage or exhort." In ancient times the word carried legal overtones, as in a legal assistant or advocate (cf. 1 John 2:1). The NIV translation "Counselor" is adequate if we keep in mind a legal counselor rather than a marriage counselor or a mental-health counselor. The Holy Spirit is the one who pleads, convinces, and instructs us. He points us to what is real and true and stands beside us as our advocate, friend, and defender.

"world"—In the context of John 14:17, the "world" refers to people who are hostile to Jesus Christ and all that he stands for. The world hates Jesus and those who follow Jesus (John 15:18). By contrast, God loved the world and sent his Son to rescue the world (John 3:16).

SCRIPTURE NOTES

¹⁶And I will ask the Father, and he will give you another

Counselor to be with you forever—¹⁷the Spirit of truth.

The world cannot accept him, because it neither sees him

nor knows him. But you know him, for he lives with you

and will be in you.

For Deeper Study

Graham, Billy. *The Holy Spirit*. Dallas: Word, 1988.

Green, Michael. *I Believe in the Holy Spirit*. Rev. ed. Grand Rapids: Eerdmans, 2004.

Keener, Craig S. *Three Crucial Questions About the Holy Spirit*. Grand Rapids: Baker, 1996.

Morris, Leon. *The Gospel According to John*. Rev. ed. New International Commentary on the New Testament. Grand Rapids: Eerdmans, 1995.

Crossing the Bridge

What biblical principles do you see in John 14:16–17?

- "Counselor" indicates that the Holy Spirit is our advocate and defender.
- The Spirit is given by the Father to those who follow the Son.
-
-
-
-
-

So What?

1. Reread the passages from John 14–16, and make a list of all that Jesus said the Holy Spirit would do.

2. How have you experienced the ministry of the Holy Spirit in your life?

3. How do you want the Spirit to work in your life in the near future?

4. Would you rather be an original disciple who had the privilege of walking and talking with Jesus or a disciple today who is permanently indwelt by the Holy Spirit? (Not that we have a choice, but it's fun to think about.)

5. Of all the biblical principles that you identified in "Crossing the Bridge," which is most applicable for you right now? Why?

Follow the Leader

Walking by the Spirit

God kept his promise and poured out his Spirit on his people at Pentecost. Since that time, God's Holy Spirit has dwelt within individual Christ followers. The Spirit supplies boldness, produces spiritual fruit, helps us resist temptation, assures us that we belong to Christ, inspires true worship, convicts us of sin, guides us into truth, forms us into a community, gifts us for ministry, and in many other ways continues the ministry of Jesus. We no longer have to meet God at the temple to experience his presence. God now lives among his people. This study focuses on our need to allow the Holy Spirit to carry out his ministry in our lives. God wants to be our source of strength and joy. He wants to deliver us from temptation and make us more like Christ, but we have to let him work in us. This calls us to the habit of walking by the Spirit.

You cannot become a Christian apart from the work of the Holy Spirit. The Christian life begins with the Spirit. Jesus himself said that "no one can enter the kingdom of God unless he is born of water and the Spirit" (John 3:5; cf. 3:8). Paul speaks of those who are "born by the power of the Spirit" (Gal. 4:29; cf. 4:6). Do you remember the critical time in your life when you were born of the Spirit?

The Christian life begins with the Holy Spirit, but sometimes we forget that the Christian life continues in just the same way. In his letter to the Galatians, Paul is dealing with a group of people who are dangerously close to forgetting that just as we are born of the Spirit, so also we go on living by the Spirit. Paul confronts them honestly about this deadly way of thinking: "Are you so foolish? After beginning with the Spirit, are you now trying to attain your goal by human effort [the flesh]?" (Gal. 3:3). Thank God that we don't bear the burden of finishing what he started. It's not that God begins our Christian life and then it's up to us to finish it. No, not at all. We have the privilege of relying on the Spirit to complete what he began in our lives. What a relief! Just as we trusted

THE POWER OF WORDS

"live"—This command in 5:16 could be translated "walk" (NASB). We often speak of our Christian "walk" as a metaphor for our way of life, and that's how the word is used here. Paul is commanding the Galatians (and us) to choose a certain way of life that relies on the Spirit.

"flesh"—In this context, the "flesh" is not referring to the human body. Our physical bodies can be used for good or bad, but the Bible doesn't teach that they are innately evil. The "flesh" here refers to human nature in its fallen state (NIV: "sinful nature"). Flesh stands in opposition to Spirit just as autonomous, self-reliant human beings stand against God. When we follow the "flesh," we pretend to be our own god and act as if the one, true God did not exist. People who follow the flesh will either become focused on religious rules resulting in legalism (the Galatians) or abandon rules altogether resulting in libertinism (the Corinthians). The flesh represents our tendency to do life apart from God.

"keep in step with"—This is a military expression that portrays soldiers marching in a straight line. The Spirit leads and we follow. It takes discipline and concentration to pay attention to the Spirit above the competing voices and follow in his footsteps. We do not have to achieve grace; we are commanded to follow.

God's work in Christ to give us new life in the first place, so we can trust God's work through the Holy Spirit to grow us up and make us more like Jesus. The question is, how do we let the Spirit do his important work?

Our focal text is from Galatians 5:16 and 25, but we can't understand the specific verses without seeing the larger picture. Paul brought the good news of Christ to the Galatians and later learned that they were being hounded by false teachers. The false teachers were saying to the Galatians: "If you want to be first-rate Christians, full-fledged Christians, real Christians, then you need to supplement your new faith in Christ with a few important Jewish rules such as eating particular foods, observing special days, and submitting to certain religious rituals, especially circumcision." You can imagine how confused these Galatians had become. Why do you suppose new converts often feel attracted to rule-oriented religion?

- It just feels safer.
- It offers tangible, measurable results.
- They hope the additional rules will help them conquer the flesh.
- It's much less complicated, and they prefer to keep it simple.
-
-

Paul calls this "Jesus-plus" message a "different gospel" since it brings spiritual slavery rather than real freedom—"I am astonished that you are so quickly deserting the one who called you by the grace of Christ and are turning to a different gospel—which is really no gospel at all" (Gal. 1:6–7a). Paul writes his letter to the Galatians to condemn the false teaching and to persuade these new believers to continue in the true gospel—trusting Christ and following the Holy Spirit. Here is how Paul's line of argument flows through the last part of Galatians:

➡ Jesus set you free from the obligation to keep the law. (5:1, 13a)
➡ But you are not free in Christ to indulge your flesh. (5:13b, 15, 26)
➡ Rather, you are free to love one another. (5:13b)
➡ Why is love so important? Because love fulfills the law (the reason you were attracted to this false teaching in the first place; it seemed more spiritual). (5:14)
➡ OK, so love fulfills the law. How do we love?
➡ You follow the Holy Spirit, who creates love! (5:16–18, 25)
➡ We need specifics. Show us what a flesh life looks like in contrast to a Spirit life.
  - When you are indulging the flesh, your life will look more like 5:19–21.
  - When you are following the Spirit, your life will look more like 5:22–24 and 6:1–10.

There is a wealth of spiritual truth in Galatians 5:1–6:10. Take a moment and read this passage if you haven't already. Now do something creative. Use the space below to summarize in your own words Paul's line of argument explained on the previous page.

A Closer Look—Galatians 5:16, 25

In light of the context, look carefully at the two verses below. Underline each command. Double underline the basis of each command (if there is one). Circle repeated words. Bracket off results or promises. Read about significant words in the sidebar on page 38. Make other observations and ask questions in the margins.

SCRIPTURE NOTES

¹⁶So I say, live [walk] by the Spirit, and you will not gratify

the desires of the sinful nature [flesh]. . . . ²⁵Since we live by

the Spirit, let us keep in step with the Spirit.

Crossing the Bridge

What biblical principles do you see in Galatians 5:16, 25 or any other place in the larger context of Galatians 5–6? The first two are done for you.

- The law shows us what is right (i.e., God's standard), but only Christ can set us free and only the Spirit can give us the power to live up to that standard.

- In "following the leader" I am both passive ("led by" in 5:18) and active ("walk by" in 5:16).

-

-

-

-

So What?

1. What do you think about the idea of "grieving the Spirit"? From the examples surrounding Ephesians 4:30, what are the most common ways that you grieve the Spirit?

2. Read "Grammar Matters!" in the sidebar. If the promise is absolute when the condition is met (i.e., *if* we follow the Spirit, we will *never* gratify the flesh), then what should our strategy be for conquering the flesh? How does this compare to our typical strategy?

3. How is following the Spirit more adventuresome and daring than trying to keep the law?

4. How do you discern the Spirit's "voice" in order to march in a straight line behind him?

5. What specific things do you need to do or avoid doing in order to stay more in step with the Spirit?

What's Growing On?

Fruit of the Spirit

When we begin a relationship with Jesus Christ, we are in reality "born of the Spirit" (John 3:5–8). God wants our new life to continue the same way it began. He wants us to "walk by the Spirit." It's not that God begins our Christian life and then it's up to us to finish it. He wants us to rely on him to complete what he started. We do this by refusing to reduce our new relationship to nothing more than a set of religious rules. The law has no power to tame the flesh (our inclination to do life apart from God). But when we discern the Spirit's voice and follow him, it will be totally and absolutely impossible for us to gratify the flesh at the same time. As we grow in the habit of staying in step with the Spirit, our lives begin to resemble Christ himself. This Christ "look" is best portrayed by the fruit-of-the-Spirit list in Galatians 5, the focus of Becoming 2.

As we talked about in Believing 2, when people become Christ followers, God takes up residence within them in the person of the Holy Spirit. Paul summarizes:

And you also were included in Christ when you heard the word of truth, the gospel of your salvation. Having believed, you were marked in him with a seal, the promised Holy Spirit, who is a deposit guaranteeing our inheritance until the redemption of those who are God's possession—to the praise of his glory. (Eph. 1:13–14)

This complex, life-changing event includes hearing the gospel, believing, being included in Christ, and being sealed with the Holy Spirit. (Sometimes the New Testament uses the phrase "baptism in the Spirit" to refer to what happens to a person at conversion.) At the end of that same letter to the

Try Your Hand at Bible Translation

Think about the following characteristics of Paul's command in Ephesians 5:18 to "be filled":

- Present tense—ongoing or repeated filling
- Imperative mood—a command to be carrried out
- Passive voice—allowing God to fill us
- Plural—not just for "super-Christians" but for all obedient believers

With these things in mind, how would you translate the second part of Ephesians 5:18?

"Keep on . . .

Ephesians, however, Paul speaks about another ministry of the Holy Spirit—the fullness of the Spirit:

> Be very careful, then, how you live—not as unwise but as wise, making the most of every opportunity, because the days are evil.
>
> Therefore do not be foolish, but understand what the Lord's will is.
>
> Do not get drunk on wine, which leads to debauchery. Instead, be filled with the Spirit. Speak to one another with psalms, hymns and spiritual songs. Sing and make music in your heart to the Lord, always giving thanks to God the Father for everything, in the name of our Lord Jesus Christ. Submit to one another out of reverence for Christ. (Eph. 5:15–21)

As Paul describes how Christians should live, he uses three statements, each having two parts—"do not do this, . . . but do that." The third statement tells us not to get drunk on wine, which leads to out-of-control, destructive living, but to be filled with the Spirit. A person who is filled with the Spirit will be a person of worship, community, joy, gratitude, and relational humility.

Being filled with the Spirit (Eph. 5) is really about the same thing as walking by the Spirit (Gal. 5). It's not that you get more of the Spirit, but that the Spirit gets more of you. To get a better sense of what it means to live a Spirit-filled life, we need to look at the context of Galatians 5:22–24, our focal passage for this study.

We see from Galatians 5:16–21 that the Holy Spirit and the flesh have declared war on each other. These two opposing powers produce in their followers a distinct character or way of life. What is allowed to reign in a person's heart will eventually work its way out to that person's behavior and will be plain for all to see. Paul makes it clear that the flesh (sinful nature) results in a chaotic existence (better described as death than life) that can be divided into several categories: (1) *sexual sins*—sexual immorality, impurity, debauchery; (2) *false religion*—idolatry, witchcraft; (3) *sins against the community*—hatred, discord, jealousy, fits of rage, selfish ambition, dissensions, factions, envy; and (4) *pagan living*—drunkenness, orgies, and the like. Paul warns that "those who live like this will not inherit the kingdom of God" (5:21). In contrast, the Spirit life looks totally different.

A Closer Look—Galatians 5:22–24

Look carefully at the verses on the next page. Mark your observations (lists, explanations, results, etc.). Read about significant words in the text below the verses. Think also about how this virtue list differs radically from the vice list that precedes it.

²²But the fruit of the Spirit is love, joy, peace, patience, kindness, goodness, faithfulness, ²³gentleness and self-control. Against such things there is no law. ²⁴Those who belong to Christ Jesus have crucified the sinful nature with its passions and desires.

1. Paul may be "holding the mirror up to the Galatians" by contrasting the sins against the community that occur in the middle of the flesh list (Gal. 5:20–21) with the fruit of the Spirit. Can you match vices and virtues that appear to be opposites?

Hatred	Love
Discord	Joy
Jealousy	Peace
Fits of rage	Patience
Selfish ambition	Kindness
Dissensions	Goodness
Factions	Faithfulness
Envy	Gentleness
	Self-control

2. Consider the meaning of each term in the fruit list. Think honestly about your life and relationships and how they match up to what the Spirit desires.

   • **Love** (*agapē*)—Love heads the list of qualities because it is a reflection of the very nature of God. All other virtues flow out of love, which is much more than tolerance or sentiment. Love is a commitment to do what God thinks is best for another person. See 1 Corinthians 13 for a full description.
   • **Joy** (*chara*)—More than human happiness, joy is a settled excitement that results from healthy relationships, including our relationship with God. Joy originates, not from immediate circumstances or passing pleasures, but from the Spirit.
   • **Peace** (*eirēnē*)—More than the absence of conflict, peace is a deep contentment and wholeness that comes from harmonious relationships.

Lights Without Electricity

Imagine visiting a town at night that appears to have no lights, no televisions—not even alarm clocks. And then imagine learning that the town's power supply is virtually infinite, but that no one in the town had thought to turn any of their electrical appliances on. Wouldn't that town seem like a silly place to you? Yet the Church is all too often like that town. God has given us the power of His Spirit to fulfill His mission in the world, yet few Christians have even begun to depend on His power.

—Craig Keener,
Three Crucial Questions, 17

—The "works" of the flesh are plural, reflecting the chaotic and disjointed nature of evil. In contrast, we do not read about the "works" of the Spirit, but about the "fruit" of the Spirit. "Fruit" is singular, reflecting the unity and harmony of God's work in our lives. Fruit is something that the Spirit grows or produces in us as we cooperate with him. It represents character qualities born out in our attitudes and actions. To put it another way, the fruit of the Spirit is a picture of what it means to be like Jesus.

"have crucified the sinful nature [flesh]"—This past-tense statement probably refers to our conversion and baptism, when we publicly identified with Christ. A common baptism confession goes like this:

Do you turn to Christ?
I turn to Christ.
Do you repent of your sins?
I repent of my sins.
Do you renounce evil?
I renounce evil.

This is when we initially said "no" to evil and "yes" to Christ. As the flesh and the Spirit battle, we must return to the promise we made at our baptism. Having been buried and raised with Christ (Gal. 2:20), we continue to crucify the flesh. Our lifelong commitment is not to negotiate with the flesh, but to continuously crucify the flesh as a part of walking by the Spirit.

- **Patience** (*makrothymia*)—The word is also translated "long-suffering." It refers to the patient enduring of some wrong without taking revenge or responding in anger. This generosity of heart calls us to bear with one another when irritated or provoked rather than to retaliate.
- **Kindness** (*chrēstotēs*)—Kindness is a sweet and gracious disposition toward others.
- **Goodness** (*agathōsynē*)—This is the outworking of the attitude of kindness in doing good to others in practical and generous ways.
- **Faithfulness** (*pistis*)—Faithfulness refers to the quality of loyalty and trustworthiness in relationships. When we are faithful, rather than being fickle or foolish, we can be counted on to keep our commitments.
- **Gentleness** (*prautēs*)—The word also is translated "meekness." As the opposite of arrogance and selfish ambition, gentleness refers to a humble submission to the Spirit that leads us to consider the needs and hurts of others ahead of our personal desires. Only a secure strength can act patiently and mildly toward others.
- **Self-control** (*ekkrateia*)—This is the opposite of self-indulgence. This quality refers to the strength and discipline (that comes from the Spirit) to control our passions and resist temptation.

No wonder Paul says that "against such things there is no law" (5:23). When we try to live up to a list of religious rules, we fail because we are relying on our own human ability. When we allow the Spirit to fill us and lead us, the Spirit produces a certain kind of life. The Spirit-led life is not a violation of the law. Rather, those who walk by the Spirit fulfill the law.

So What?

1. Has the Holy Spirit been over- or underemphasized in your church experience? (Some might want to say that the Spirit has been properly emphasized.) What do you think you have missed if you have not been getting balanced teaching on the Spirit?

2. How would you translate Ephesians 5:18? Why is this verse crucial to a proper understanding of the Holy Spirit?

3. As you think about the fruit list, which ones most characterize your life? Which ones least characterize your life?

4. Again, thinking about the fruit list, when has the Spirit been allowed to produce his fruit in greatest abundance in your life? In other words, in what kind of life seasons or situations are you walking by the Spirit most faithfully?

5. What are some practical things that help you to crucify the flesh?

6. Chapter 2 has focused on the Holy Spirit. What has been most helpful and meaningful to you from this chapter?

Don't Pull Out the Nails

The first great secret of holiness lies in the degree and the decisiveness of our repentance. If besetting sins persistently plague us, it is either because we have never truly repented, or because, having repented, we have not maintained our repentance. It is as if, having nailed our old nature to the cross, we keep wistfully returning to the scene of its execution. We begin to fondle it, to caress it, to long for its release, even to try to take it down again from the cross. We need to learn to leave it there. When some jealous, or proud, or malicious, or impure thought invades our mind we must kick it out at once. It is fatal to begin to examine it and consider whether we are going to give in to it or not. We have declared war on it; we are not going to resume negotiations. . . . We have crucified the flesh; we are never going to [with]draw the nails.

—John Stott,
Message of Galatians, 151–52

For Deeper Study

Fung, Ronald Y. K. *The Epistle to the Galatians.* New International Commentary on the New Testament. Grand Rapids: Eerdmans, 1988.

Hansen, G. Walter. *Galatians.* IVP New Testament Commentary. Downers Grove, IL: InterVarsity Press, 1994.

Stott, John R. W. *Baptism and Fullness: The Work of the Holy Spirit Today.* Downers Grove, IL: InterVarsity Press, 1975.

Stott, John R. W. *The Message of Galatians.* The Bible Speaks Today. Downers Grove, IL: InterVarsity Press, 1968.

The People of God

The Church

Are you trying to live the Christian life all by yourself?

We cannot live the Christian life in isolation, like some religious Robinson Crusoe. Membership in the church is not an optional extra. The fact is, we cannot be fully Christian without belonging to the church. As we study the New Testament we find that to be a Christian is to be "in Christ," and that this means being a member of a new society of which Christ is the living Head—the church. The New Testament knows nothing of unattached Christians. Consider the matter in a more mundane way. What would we think of a man who said that he wanted to be a soldier but insisted that he could be a perfectly good one without joining the army? An unattached soldier is nonsense—and so is the notion of a solitary Christian. (Shelley, *Theology for Ordinary People*, 146)

The necessity of community is not something that comes naturally for Christians living in an individualistic culture. Some of us have to learn the hard way. When we pull away from church or when we neglect church, we are the ones who suffer. We grow cold and loveless. Relating to God means relating to the people of God. We need each other. In Believing 3 we will focus on the church: Christ's body and bride, the Spirit's temple, and the Father's family.

In the New Testament, the word for "church" is *ekklēsia*, meaning "called out ones." This important word describes a community of people from every tribe, language, people, and nation that belongs to Jesus Christ, the head of the church. Most of the time the word *ekklēsia* refers to a *local community* of those who profess allegiance to Christ and gather regularly for the purpose of worship and fellowship (e.g., "the church in Corinth" or "the church in Philippi"). At other times, the word depicts the *universal church*—all believers across the world and throughout the ages (e.g., Eph. 5:25: "Christ loved the church and gave himself up for her"). One thing is certain, an *ekklēsia* (church) was not just a civic association or religious club, but a community called out by God. As Bruce Shelley puts it, "The church . . . is more than an aggregation—people who have chosen to come together. It is a congregation, a people called together" by God (*Theology for Ordinary People*, 139). The church is not merely an organization or an institution providing religious programs or a place to find help in your individual walk with God. The church is not a building; it is people. The church is a spiritual organism, a living reality that draws its life from the very life of the triune God, the perfect community.

To grasp the New Testament concept of church, we need to look beyond the word *ekklēsia* to the central images or word pictures of the church. There are many such images (one writer lists over a hundred), but we will spend a few minutes with four main ones. I could tell you about these, but it will mean more to you if you discover them for yourself. Look up the key verses for each image and write a brief summary of what each image signifies and why it is important for our understanding of church.

- Body of Christ (Rom. 12:4–5; 1 Cor. 12:12–27; Eph. 3:6; 5:23; Col. 1:18–24; 2:19; 3:15)

- Bride of Christ (Eph. 5:25, 27, 31–32; Rev. 19:7; 21:2; 22:17)

- Temple of the Spirit (1 Cor. 3:16–17; 2 Cor. 6:16; Eph. 2:21–22; Heb. 3:6; 10:21; 1 Peter 2:5; Rev. 21:2–3, 10–22)

- Household/Family of God (Gal. 6:10; Eph. 2:19; 3:15; 1 Tim. 3:15; Heb. 2:11; 1 Peter 4:17)

A Closer Look—1 Peter 2:4–10

Our focal passage is one of the most profound passages on the church in the New Testament. Take time to dig deep into this text. Mark up the passage with your observations. Look for important words, lists, contrasts, comparisons, purpose statements, significant phrases, figures of speech, conjunctions, emotional terms, time indicators, and so on. Before you can know what the Bible means, you need to observe what it says.

A Mosaic

Community is like a large mosaic. Each little piece seems so insignificant. One piece is bright red, another cold blue or dull green, another warm purple, another sharp yellow, another shining gold. Some look precious, others ordinary. Some look valuable, others worthless. Some look gaudy, others delicate. As individual stones, we can do little with them except compare them and judge their beauty and value. When, however, all these little stones are brought together in one big mosaic portraying the face of Christ, who would ever question the importance of any one of them? If one of them, even the least spectacular one, is missing, the face is incomplete. Together in the one mosaic, each little stone is indispensable and makes a unique contribution to the glory of God. That's community, a fellowship of little people who together make God visible in the world.

—Henri Nouwen,
Only Necessary Thing, 124

Life Without Church?

The virtuous soul that is alone . . . is like a burning coal that is alone. It will grow colder rather than hotter.

—St. John of the Cross,
quoted in Philip Yancey, *Church*, 23

⁴As you come to him, the living Stone—rejected by men but chosen by God and precious to him—⁵you also, like living stones, are being built into a spiritual house to be a holy priesthood, offering spiritual sacrifices acceptable to God through Jesus Christ. ⁶For in Scripture it says: "See, I lay a stone in Zion, a chosen and precious cornerstone, and the one who trusts in him will never be put to shame" [Isa. 28:16]. . . . ⁹But you are a chosen people, a royal priesthood, a holy nation, a people belonging to God, that you may declare the praises of him who called you out of darkness into his wonderful light. ¹⁰Once you were not a people, but now you are the people of God; once you had not received mercy, but now you have received mercy.

THE POWER OF WORDS

"the living Stone"—Jesus was compared to food in 2:3, but now he is identified as a stone—the stone that the human builders rejected and crucified. To God, however, this "Stone" is precious. Rather than being a lifeless thing like a normal rock, Jesus has been raised from the dead and is the "living Stone" (see 1 Peter 1:18–21).

"a spiritual house"—The Rock (Jesus) is building a new house, a spiritual temple where God will live. This house is made up of "living stones"—people who belong to Jesus. As living stones connected to the living Stone, we are part of a community where God himself lives through his Spirit.

"spiritual sacrifices"—This term refers to the offering of ourselves to God (cf. Rom. 12:1). We offer to God our praise (cf. Heb. 13:15–16) and our service (e.g., Phil. 4:18). God desires both our words of worship and our acts of service. Also, spiritual sacrifices (those that honor the Holy Spirit) should be offered with the proper motives and attitudes.

Crossing the Bridge

What biblical principles do you see in 1 Peter 2:4–10?

- Since we experience biblical community "through Jesus Christ" (v. 5), we need to see Christ as the true source of genuine community and not try to generate community around any other source.

-

-

-

So What?

1. Do you really think church is essential to the Christian life? Why or why not?

2. What place does church hold right now in your life? Do you need to make any changes?

BELIEVING 3—*The Church*

3. Many of us have grown up in a culture that prizes the individual and emphasizes self-sufficiency above the community. How has this individualistic culture affected your approach to church?

4. Which of the four central images of the church is most meaningful to you at this time in your life? Why?

5. What small step could your church take to encourage genuine community?

6. How could you participate in making this happen?

"cornerstone"—In an ancient building the cornerstone was a very large and costly stone that anchored the entire structure. This massive foundation stone bound together different rows of stones and provided strength and precision for the rest of the building. As a spiritual house or temple, God's people are built upon Jesus, the precious cornerstone (see Eph. 2:20).

The Future of the Church
The future of the church depends on whether it develops true community. We can get by for a while on size, skilled communication, and programs to meet every need, but unless we sense that we belong to each other, with masks off, the vibrant church of today will become the powerless church of tomorrow.

—Larry Crabb in foreword to Randy Frazee, *Connecting Church*, 13

Cross-References
Matt. 16:13–20; 18:15–17; Acts 1–2, 10–11; Rom. 12:3–8; 1 Cor. 1:10–17; 3:1–17; 12:12–27; 14:1–40; 2 Cor. 6:16; Eph. 1:22–23; 2:11–22; 3:6–11; 4:3–16; 5:23, 25–27, 31–32; Col. 1:15–24; 2:19; 1 Tim. 3:1–13, 15; Titus 1:5–9; Heb. 3:6; 10:19–25; Rev. 2–3; 19:1–9; 21:1–27; 22:17

For Deeper Study
Banks, Robert. *Paul's Idea of Community.* Rev. ed. Peabody, MA: Hendrickson, 1994.
Gibbs, Eddie. *ChurchNext.* Downers Grove, IL: InterVarsity Press, 2000.
Stanley, Andy, and Bill Willits. *Creating Community.* Sisters, OR: Multnomah, 2004.
Wilson, Jonathon R. *Why Church Matters: Worship, Ministry, and Mission in Practice.* Grand Rapids: Baker, 2006.
Yancey, Philip. *Church: Why Bother?* Grand Rapids: Zondervan, 1998.

Personal Glory or Kingdom Greatness?

Serving

Although our culture says that life should revolve around the individual, God reminds us that when we enter a relationship with Jesus Christ, we become part of Christ's body, the church. We cannot experience the Christian life in isolation from other Christians. We are a "chosen people, a royal priesthood, a holy nation, a people belonging to God, that [we] may declare the praises of him who called [us] out of darkness into his wonderful light" (1 Peter 2:9). Once we were a bunch of scattered loners, but now, by the grace of Jesus Christ, we are the people of God. We have been called together (or congregated) in Christ. We don't have to go it alone. We get to experience life in community, and this life flows from the triune God, the perfect community.

Being a member of the people of God is not only a privilege; it is also a responsibility. In Behaving 3 we will concentrate on our need to serve each other. As members of Christ's body, we are called to meet each other's needs through acts of practical service. As "living stones" in God's spiritual house, we offer spiritual sacrifices—not only to praise God but also to minister to other members of God's family.

Rusty Stevens, a ministry leader who lives in Virginia Beach, Virginia, tells this story:

As I feverishly pushed the lawn mower around our yard, I wondered if I'd finish before dinner. Mikey, our 6-year-old, walked up and, without even asking, stepped in front of me and placed his hands on the mower handle. Knowing that he wanted to help me, I quit pushing.

The mower quickly slowed to a stop. Chuckling inwardly at his struggles, I resisted the urge to say, "Get out of here kid. You're in my way," and said instead, "Here, son. I'll help you." As I resumed pushing, I bowed my back and leaned forward, and walked spread-legged to avoid colliding with Mikey. The grass cutting continued, but more slowly, and less efficiently than before, because Mikey was "helping" me.

Suddenly, tears came to my eyes as it hit me: *This is the way my heavenly Father allows me to "help" him build his kingdom!* I pictured my heavenly Father at work seeking, saving, and transforming people, and there I was, with my weak hands "helping." My Father *could* do the work by himself, but he doesn't. He chooses to stoop gracefully to allow me to co-labor with him. Why? For *my* sake, because he wants me to have the privilege of ministering with him. (Larson, *Illustrations*, 153)

Although God allows us to "help" him by allowing us to serve others, we sometimes have trouble accepting service as a divine opportunity. The first disciples had the same struggle, as we will see from the focal passage in Mark 10. Sadly, in the mirror of their lust for power, selfish ambition, inflated egos, and spiritual ignorance, we sometimes see our own reflection.

A Closer Look—Mark 10:35–45

One of the best ways to get inside a story is to ask the typical story questions: Who? What? When? Where? Why? and How? Find Mark 10:35–45 in your Bible. In the space below answer the questions about Jesus' teaching on kingdom greatness. One of the boxes has been done for you. Once you've experienced a story by looking at it from all angles, you will never again be content to "skim" a story (e.g., notice the contrast between vv. 35 and 45).

WHO?	WHAT?

"the cup . . . the baptism"—Jesus mentions drinking a cup and being baptized with a baptism in Mark 10:38. These words are metaphors for suffering. In Gethsemane Jesus would pray, "Take this cup from me" (Mark 14:36) when referring to his impending suffering and death. He also refers to these events as his "baptism" (Luke 12:50). When Jesus asks James and John if they can drink the cup and undergo the baptism, they flippantly answer, "We can." The truth is that they have not yet connected greatness in the kingdom with suffering. Glory and suffering go together (Rom. 8:17).

"ransom"—In ancient writings this term referred to the payment made to free a slave or a prisoner (i.e., the price of release). Ransom is tied to the cost of life and freedom. Jesus gave his life "in place of" or "instead of" the many. Jesus substituted himself for the many. We should have died because of our sins, but he died in our place. Here we see the ultimate form of service.

chart continued on next page...

WHEN?	WHERE?
	James and John approach Jesus, apart from the other disciples, in order to get something (v. 35).
	James and John desire to sit on Jesus' "right and left" when he comes into his glory (vv. 37, 40). Check out Mark 15:27, the only other place where these same words occur in Mark.
	The places of honor (v. 40).
	The ten other disciples got close enough to hear Jesus' response (v. 41).
	Jesus called everybody together (v. 42).
	The Son of Man (Jesus) comes to human beings (v. 45). Notice how Jesus' "approach" to serve as a ransom (v. 45) differs radically from the approach of James and John to secure worldly glory (v. 35).

WHY?	HOW?

A Real Servant?

A wise person once said that you will know whether you are a servant by how you respond when you are treated like one.

Crossing the Bridge

What biblical principles do you see in Mark 10:35–45? Below are two examples to get you started.

- We should beware of uncritically embracing pagan models of greatness.

- Jesus was willing to oppose popular expectations about servanthood in order to be a true servant. The religious culture of that time expected a Messiah that would conquer the Romans and establish an earthly kingdom. Jesus came as a "suffering Messiah" for the purpose of establishing an eternal kingdom.

-

BEHAVING 3—*Serving*

Since service strongly relates to our motives, Richard Foster's distinction between "self-righteous service" and "true service" is insightful and convicting (*Celebration of Discipline*, 128–30):

• *Self-righteous service* comes through human effort. It expends immense amounts of energy calculating and scheming about how to render service. *True service*, however, comes from our relationship with God, from divine promptings and urgings.

• *Self-righteous service* is impressed with the "big deal," whereas *true service* finds it almost impossible to distinguish the small from the large service.

• *Self-righteous service* requires external rewards, but *true service* is content with remaining hidden from the spotlight.

• *Self-righteous service* is concerned with results and becomes bitter if expectations are not met, while *true service* is free from the need to measure results.

• *Self-righteous service* picks and chooses whom to serve, favoring the high and powerful. *True service*, on the other hand, does not discriminate in its ministry.

• *Self-righteous service* is affected by moods and whims, serving only when the feelings are present. *True service* knows it can't depend on feelings and ministers faithfully because there is a need.

• *Self-righteous service* is temporary, resting easy after the service has been performed. By contrast, *true service* is a lifestyle and mind-set.

• *Self-righteous service* centers on glorifying the individual and spoils community. *True service* builds community by genuinely caring for the needs of others.

So What?

1. How does the story in Mark 10:35–45 affect your understanding of and commitment to being a servant?

Cross-References
Matt. 20:20–28; John 13:1–17; Acts 6:1–6; Rom. 12:11; 1 Cor. 12:5; 2 Cor. 4:5; 13:4; Gal. 1:10; 6:2; Eph. 4:12; Phil. 2:1–11; Col. 3:23–24; James 1:27; 1 Peter 4:10

For Deeper Study
Berding, Kenneth A. *What Are Spiritual Gifts? Rethinking the Conventional View.* Grand Rapids: Kregel, 2006.
Bugbee, Bruce. *What You Do Best in the Body of Christ.* Rev. and exp. Grand Rapids: Zondervan, 2005.
Garland, David E. *Mark.* NIV Application Commentary. Grand Rapids: Zondervan, 1996.

2. Why do you suppose that Jesus chooses service to define greatness? In other words, why does service seem like such a big deal to God?

3. As members of his community, Christ desires that we serve each other. He allows us to "help" him by serving each other. In your life, what are the great obstacles to service?

4. Which type of "self-righteous service" mentioned by Foster is the biggest trap for you? Why?

5. What inspires and motivates you to serve?

6. What are some specific ways that we can serve each other? What are some ways we can serve people outside our community?

It's Not About Me

Humility

"Nowhere in the Great Tradition of Christianity before the twentieth century can one find the uniquely modern phenomenon of 'churchless Christianity'" (Olson, *Mosaic*, 292). Since we weren't made for "churchless Christianity," we will suffer more than we can imagine if we neglect God's provision of church. We were created for community, and if we really believe that we are relationally connected to other members of the body of Christ and are part of the same family, then we will make each other a priority. We will serve each other. John Ortberg is on target when he says that "authentic community is characterized perhaps more than anything else by mutual servanthood and submission" (*Life You've Always Wanted*, 111). Service does something to us that nothing else can do. It frees us from the prison of being absorbed and preoccupied with ourselves. This self-forgetfulness can also be described as humility. In Becoming 3 we will see how the habit of service produces in us the quality of humility.

I t may seem strange, but getting a handle on humility begins by understanding its opposite—pride. "Pride is spiritual cancer," writes C. S. Lewis in his remarkable chapter on "The Great Sin" in *Mere Christianity* (pages 109–14). Pride, he says, is "the essential vice, the utmost evil." It leads to every other sin because it is the "complete anti-God state of mind."

How do you know if you are a proud person? Lewis offers a reliable test—the more pride we have, the more we will dislike it in other people because pride is "essentially competitive." Pride is like playing a game in which we invent the rules and rig the outcome so that we always win. Anyone who has more influence or ability or money or brains (or anything) than I have, is my enemy. Pride sets out to defeat the rival through an all-out competition.

Subject or Object?
How many times in the story does the Pharisee appear as the subject in his own statements?

Notice that the only time the tax collector mentions himself, he is the object.

The worst part is that pride can creep right into the center of our religious lives. Lewis warns, "Whenever we find that our religious life is making us feel that we are good—above all, that we are better than someone else—I think we may be sure that we are being acted on, not by God, but by the devil." The very bottom of the deep, dark pride pit is where "you look down on others so much that you don't care what they think of you." Their opinion is worthless because we are so far above them that they are worthless in our eyes.

In our focal story from Luke 18, Jesus confronts those "who were confident of their own righteousness and looked down on everybody else" (v. 9). In a religious competition between the Pharisee and the tax collector, everyone would expect the Pharisee to win, but God uses a different scorecard. "In God," Lewis says, "you come up against something which is in every respect immeasurably superior to yourself. Unless you know God as that—and, therefore, know yourself as nothing in comparison—you do not know God at all."

A Closer Look—Luke 18:9–14

Locate the parable of the Pharisee and the tax collector in your Bible. Ask the standard story questions like you did with our last story: Who? What? When? Where? Why? and How? Write your answers in the boxes below. There are no shortcuts to reading a story closely. It's hard work and it takes time, but the rewards are great.

WHO?	WHAT?

WHEN?	WHERE?

WHY?	HOW?

Crossing the Bridge

Two men go up to the temple to pray—one a highly respected religious leader and the other a much-despised traitor and cheat. But something unexpected happens during this prayer time, and the story takes a surprising turn at the end. Now that you have studied the story carefully, what do you see as the main points or theological principles of the story?

"Pharisee"—The Pharisees were the most pious group of people in Jewish society. They tried to interpret the law carefully and went beyond others in applying it to every aspect of life. In their interpretation, they gave priority to the traditions of men. The people greatly respected the Pharisees as religious leaders and experts.

"tax collector"—Tax collectors were likely the most hated group in Jewish society. Since they collaborated with the occupying pagan government (Rome), they were seen as traitors. They often collected too much tax and became wealthy at the expense of the people.

"righteousness . . . evildoers . . . justified"—These words don't appear to have anything in common in English, but they do in Greek. They are all built on the same root (-δικ). What difference does this make? Jesus tells the parable to confront those who are confident of their own "righteousness" and look down on everybody else. The Pharisee boasts that he is not an "evildoer" or "unjust" like other people. But because the Pharisee's heart is full of pride, the humble tax collector is the one who goes home "justified." The Pharisee goes home unjustified (i.e., as an evildoer), the very condition he claimed did not apply to him. This little wordplay sums up the whole story.

- Religious activity such as prayer, fasting, and tithing does not guarantee that a person is closely connected to God.

- When it comes to right standing before God, the standard is not a human one, but a heavenly one.

-

-

-

Cultivating Humility

Often stories in the Gospels send a message by how they are connected to surrounding stories. The story that comes right before our focal story is about an unjust judge and a widow (Luke 18:1–8). That story highlights the widow's persevering faith and ends with a question: "When the Son of Man comes, will he find faith on the earth?" You can almost hear the Pharisees answer, "Well, of course he will find faith on the earth, and he will find it among us, the Pharisees. We are the faithful ones." Jesus then tells the parable of 18:9–14 to show that there are some surprises when it comes to who has faith and who doesn't. God puts a premium on humility. Notice also the episode that follows our focal story. As people bring their children to Jesus, he uses this as an object lesson of real faith—"anyone who will not receive the kingdom of God like a little child will never enter it" (Luke 18:17). The simple, humble, sincere faith of a child stands alongside the humble faith of a repentant tax collector and in contrast to the proud "faith" of the overconfident and arrogant Pharisee.

The problem then is pride, and the solution is humility. Humility is having a healthy, realistic view of ourselves, of others, and of God. It is realizing that God is God and we are not. Humility means that we focus on others rather than on ourselves, not that we draw even more attention to ourselves by pretending to be worthless nobodies. So how do we cultivate humility? The first step is to admit that we are proud (not a small step). Foster suggests the next step:

> More than any other single way, the grace of humility is worked into our lives through . . . service. Humility, as we all know, is one of those virtues that is never gained by seeking it. The more we pursue it the more distant it becomes. To think we have it is sure evidence that we don't. Therefore, most of us assume there is nothing we can do to gain this prized Christian virtue, and so we do nothing. But there is something we can do. . . . Service is the most conducive to the growth of humility. When we set out on a consciously chosen course of action that accents the good of others

and is, for the most part, a hidden work, a deep change occurs in our spirits. (*Celebration of Discipline*, 130)

So What?

1. Most of us have a lot to learn about humility. What have you learned about pride and humility in Becoming 3? How can you begin to apply what you have learned?

2. Do you tend toward "low pride" (pretending that you are nothing) or "high pride" (pretending that you are everything)? Explain your answer.

3. Can you think of some ways that we use religious activity to cover up a prideful heart? (Remember that pious practices are not inherently evil since the tax collector also goes to the temple to pray.)

4. As you think about times in your life when you have served, how does the practice of service seem to change you?

Humility: What It Is and Isn't

Humility is not about convincing ourselves—or others—that we are unattractive or incompetent. It is not about "beating ourselves up" or trying to make ourselves nothing. If God wanted to make us nothing, he could have done it.

Humility has to do with a submitted willingness. It involves a healthy self-forgetfulness. We will know we have begun to make progress in humility when we find that we get so enabled by the Holy Spirit to live in the moment that we cease to be preoccupied with ourselves, one way or the other. When we are with others, we are truly *with* them, not wondering how they can be of benefit to us. . . . Humility involves . . . the realization that the universe does not revolve around us. . . . Humility is the freedom to stop trying to be what we're not, or pretending to be what we're not and accepting our "appropriate smallness."

—John Ortberg,
Life You've Always Wanted, 102–3

Cross-References

Deut. 8:11–18; 2 Chron. 7:14; Pss. 18:27; 147:6; Prov. 3:34; Isa. 57:15; 66:2; Matt. 23:12; Luke 14:11; Phil. 2:1–11; James 4:10; 1 Peter 5:5–7

For Deeper Study

Bock, Darrell L. *Luke.* NIV Application Commentary. Grand Rapids: Zondervan, 1996.

Foster, Richard J. *Celebration of Discipline.* 25th anniversary ed. San Francisco: HarperSanFrancisco, 2003.

Lewis, C. S. *Mere Christianity.* New York: Macmillan, 1952.

5. It appears that we often compartmentalize service in unfair ways. For example, the people who set up chairs for a worship service or wash dishes after a church gathering are real servants, while those who pray for the gathering or write the drama script to be used during the worship time are not usually thought of as servants. Do you think we have trouble seeing the many dimensions of service? Why or why not?

6. What are some ways that you think God might be calling you to serve your community at this point in your life?

Carson, D. A. *The Farewell Discourse and the Final Prayer of Jesus*. Grand Rapids: Baker, 1988.

Dorsett, Lyle W. *Seeking the Secret Place: The Spiritual Formation of C. S. Lewis*. Grand Rapids: Baker, 2004.

Foster, Richard J. *Celebration of Discipline*. 25th anniversary ed. San Francisco: HarperSanFrancisco, 2003.

Frazee, Randy. *The Connecting Church*. Grand Rapids: Zondervan, 2001.

Graham, Billy. *The Holy Spirit*. Dallas: Word, 1988.

Hoehner, Harold W. *Ephesians*. Grand Rapids: Baker, 2002.

Keener, Craig S. *Three Crucial Questions about the Holy Spirit*. Grand Rapids: Baker, 1996.

Larson, Craig Brian, ed. *Illustrations for Preaching and Teaching*. Grand Rapids: Baker, 1993.

Lewis, C. S. *Mere Christianity*. New York: Macmillan, 1952.

Long, Jimmy. *Emerging Hope: Strategy for Reaching Postmodern Generations*. 2nd ed. Downers Grove, IL: InterVarsity Press, 2004.

Nouwen, Henri J. M. *The Only Necessary Thing*. New York: Crossroad, 1999.

Olson, Roger E. *The Mosaic of Christian Belief*. Downers Grove, IL: InterVarsity Press, 2002.

Ortberg, John. *The Life You've Always Wanted*. Grand Rapids: Zondervan, 1997.

————. *Love Beyond Reason: Moving God's Love From Your Head to Your Heart*. Grand Rapids: Zondervan, 1998.

————. "Spiritual Growth — My Job or God's?" Preaching Today tape #190, at www.preachingtodaysermons.com.

Shelley, Bruce L. *Theology for Ordinary People: What You Should Know to Make Sense Out of Life*. Downers Grove, IL: InterVarsity Press, 1993.

Smith, Gordon T. *The Voice of Jesus: Discernment, Prayer, and the Witness of the Spirit*. Downers Grove, IL: InterVarsity Press, 2003.

Stott, John R. W. *Authentic Christianity: From the Writings of John Stott*. Ed. Timothy Dudley-Smith. Downers Grove, IL: InterVarsity Press, 1996.

————. *The Cross of Christ*. Downers Grove, IL: InterVarsity Press, 1986.

————. *The Message of Galatians*. The Bible Speaks Today. Downers Grove, IL: InterVarsity Press, 1968.

Warren, Rick. *The Purpose-Driven Life*. Grand Rapids: Zondervan, 2002.

Willard, Dallas. *Renovation of the Heart*. Colorado Springs: NavPress, 2002.

Yancey, Philip. *Church: Why Bother?* Grand Rapids: Zondervan, 1998.

J Scott Duvall is professor of New Testament at Ouachita Baptist University, a Christian liberal-arts college in Arkansas, where he teaches Spiritual Formation, Interpreting the Bible, Greek, and New Testament Studies. He received his B.A. from Ouachita and his M.Div. and Ph.D. from Southwestern Seminary, and has been teaching at OBU since 1989. He also serves as copastor of Fellowship Church of Arkadelphia, Arkansas.

Duvall's other publications include *Grasping God's Word*, *Journey into God's Word*, *Preaching God's Word*, *Biblical Greek Exegesis*, *The Story of Israel*, *The Dictionary of Biblical Prophecy and End Times*, and *Experiencing God's Story of Life and Hope: A Workbook for Spiritual Formation*.